Praise for Three

"Brian R. Martens is a maste[r] [of the] [Japa]nese art form known as the h[aiku, which is short and] compact. He also writes longer poems, which give him the opportunity to explore big topics like time and space, mystery and what he calls "Vision Wind." Both haiku and longer poems are collected in a new book titled *Three Raven Gate*, published by McCaa Books, a major North Bay publisher of poetry. In an essay at the back of this book, Martens explains that he was 'hiding my voice behind other poets' and that 'revealing of my inner thoughts and life in words is my salvation and a way to befriend myself.' The poems in *Three Raven Gate* will make Martens new friends in the world of poetry and beyond. They reveal the wonders one can work with a form as short and compact a haiku, and they take readers into the immense mysteries of the human heart. The illustrations by artist Michael Hofmann—who is a master of Japanese brush painting—stand on their own. They also enhance Martens' haiku. *Three Raven Gate* is a feast for the eye and the ear."
—JONAH RASKIN. Author of *Natives, Newcomers, Exiles, Fugitives: Northern California Writers and their Work.*

"Within Brian Martens's *Three Raven Gate* a reader finds the best kind of poetry: direct experience transformed into contemplation and understanding. This fine gift of a moment's pleasure reminds us that the most admirable human activity is sharing."
—MARVIN R. HIEMSTRA. Author of *French Kiss Destiny, Poet Wrangler,* and the upcoming *Memories: Snug under a Raven's Wing.*

"Brian Martens is a myth-maker and a dreamer. He does what many poets do, looking closely at the experiences of his life to see where they open out into spaciousness. But my inner ear also caught mythic tones and dream-time themes. He weaves them together with the quotidian, and suddenly there is something shining and breathing there that gives blessing."

—SHERRIE ROSE-WALKER. Author of two chapbooks, *Two Trees* and *Celtic Ray.*

"Martens' haiku exist in that ephemeral space we seek in our daily lives."

—AMOS WHITE. Haiku poet and author of *The Sound of The Web:* Haiku poetry on Facebook and Twitter.

Three Raven Gate

Haiku & Other Poems

Brian R. Martens

Illustrations by Michael Hofmann

Three Raven Gate

Haiku & Other Poems

Brian R. Martens

Illustrations by Michael Hofmann

McCaa Books • Santa Rosa, CA

McCaa Books
1604 Deer Run
Santa Rosa, CA 95405-7535

ISBN 978-1-7337770-2-5
Library of Congress Control Number 2019913608

First published in 2019 by McCaa Books,
an imprint of McCaa Publications.

Printed in the United States of America
Typeset in Minion Pro

www.mccaabooks.com

"No two trees are the same to Raven."

—David Wagoner, from his poem "Lost"

Contents

This book is dedicated to the unfathomable
Mystery that we all live in.

HAIKU

WINTER

I
North wind of power
Winged creatures fly in presence
As winter rattles

II
Nature asks of trust
Go beyond the known, comfort
Birds trust air to fly

III
Water shifts to ice
Quantum change of properties
Change can be instant

IV
Winter darkness hides
Within shells, water houses
Light buries deeper

V
Mirrors of winter
Reflecting ancient leaves drowned
Cold silent water

VI
Head heart gut aligned
Inside prepared for the storm
Allows birds to sing

VII
Blustery old winds
Disturb calm, scatter directions
Rattling view of sky

VIII
With integration
The still voice speaks quiet truth
One's nature declares

IX
Sun recedes alone
The winds support birds away
Sounds muffled by snow

X
Standing stones, cold air
Ancient showing up foretells
Rattling seedpods

XI
Risk for decisions
Step into grace with unknown
Held with clouds as rain

XII
White settling frost
Urging mystery inward
Holding sinking in

XIII
Stones and olive trees
Seeds underground holding life
Stories unfold new

XIV
Cool tears from the sky
Sweet fog with mixed mossy stones
Thick moldy air beckons

XV
Beauty in conflict
Waves wind collide in wild awe
Together hold both

Waves wind collide in wild awe

XVI
Winter creatures fly
Power of North hides the source
Dancing rattles warm

XVII
Attitude of rain
Letting go of clouds, release
Nourishing for earth

XVIII
Power of the Great
Sparks the gap between seasons
Light and dark unfold

XIX
Deep within the well
Gratitude fusion old, new
Flowing life's river

XX

Cool rain with warm tea
Infused by thoughts of Dog nose
Sniffing dimensions

Infused by thoughts of Dog nose

XXI
Stone people melt ice
Peering into spring, what waits?
Sun calls forth action

XXII
Heavy winter death
Close, spring beckons softly now
Snow covers knowing

XXIII
Simply elegant
No extra thought, word, and deed
An untroubled stone

XXIV
Poems elevate
Birds sing all as poetry
Rising call to prayer

XXV
Expectations held
Difficult conversations
Attachments fly far

XXVI
Receding snow waits
Sun and snow announce the spring
Single songs of Birds

XXVII
Deep breaths of damp air
Holding my nature, purring
Within, moon cat eyes

Holding my nature, purring

SPRING

XXVIII
South wind carries love
Four legged healing stories
Spring journey with drum

XXIX
Spring watches winter
Waiting opportunities
Single blade of grass

XXX
Birds release grasp, fly
Air supports dream of being
Descent to earth home

XXXI
Engage and Evolve
Conversation moves heart mind
Bird songs listening

XXXII
Baby birds seek worms
No vision beyond the nest
Adults fly freely

XXXIII
Settling rainfall
Open to receive blessing
Birds feed on new worms

XXXIV
The boon comes hidden
Seeping, attached everywhere
Wren song acceptance

XXXV
Your plant is alive
Growing new from deep places
Asking for old light

XXXVI
Persistent nature
Beetle pushing the dung ball
Orient success

XXXVII
Spring trees in water
Alluvial tea soaks all
Silent birds awakes

XXXVIII
Blue Heron watches
Above fast moving water
Dreams passing under

Blue Heron watches

XXXIX
Elements from dirt
Grown into being, rootless
Hands, feet dig in dirt

XL
Seeds sown fertile soil
Sprout in new and surprised ground
Wrens follow the seeds

XLI
Seeds intelligence
Hides in earth, true to itself
Opens to the sun

XLII
Life begins as Love
Final gate is passing Love
Think Love breathe Love, air

XLIII
Sufficient the day
Animals tracking for food
Heart leading the way

Animals tracking for food

XLIV
Old stones listening
Bamboo holding family ties
Babies crawl with ants

XLV
The gap between thoughts
The pulse of the Universe
All hearts beat as one

XLVI
The new day forgets
Storms pass and the Sun returns
Fresh dew untainted

XLVII
Tears of unknowing
Bringing questions, from soft rain
Falling through windows

XLVIII
Sleeping with Angels
Soft wings intimate holding
Motherly passing

XLIX
Blackbird beaded eye
Penetrates its world with song
Reflects the joyous

L
Darkness and light merge
Crack between both worlds opens
Step into water

LI
The dream lives inside
Fed by constant inner fire
Unstoppable force

Fed by constant inner fire

LII
The Myth reconciles
Plants, animals, man, earth, join
Initiation

LIII
Nature harmony
Wren song ancient art inspire
Myths to daily life

LIV
Conflict questions bond
Fast emotions, trail of tears
Lions fight for turf

LV
Planning far ahead
Generations flourishing
Raven nesting young

LVI
Go over the hill
See new, remember the old
Engage in both worlds

LVII
The portal beckons
Opening and closing worlds
Steps taken quickly

SUMMER

LVIII
Fire rises in East
Walking the truth of vision
Sing the authentic

LIX
Taking care of self
Open to loving kindness
Purring cat grooms self

Open to loving kindness

LX
Leadership is now
No hesitation for growth
Ravens trust the day

Ravens trust the day

LXI
Life as a spiral
Learning, reflecting, growing
Breathe as air rising

LXII
Awake with fresh eyes
Every day sun rises new
Expanding the view

LXIII
Opportunity
Leap beyond hesitation
Opening flower

LXIV
Trees in the forest
Finds strength in standing alone
In community

LXV
Tall trees roots running
Water mirroring conscious
Insects on water

Tall trees roots running

LXVI
Feminine in red
Pilot of the sailing ship
Flowers in your hair

LXVII
Hummingbird of Joy
Infinite humming balance
Shows rainbow at dawn

Infinite humming balance

LXVIII
Watching blackberries you
With late sun full fluid eyes
Ripening to smiles

LXIX
Garden full of Sun
Young birds fly open to song
Heat brings to fullness

LXX
Belief beyond looks
Lion mind begets Lion
Courage to be self

LXXI
The warm evening settles
Held mothers in angel wings
Soft intimacy

LXXII
Beauty forever
Felt masking the mystery
Flower to flower

LXXIII
Summer radiance
Opening all to fullness
Lasting forever

LXXIV
Star night unconscious
Through creative intention
Imagine your way

Star night unconscious

LXXV
Edgy summer heat
Sprays growth from soils crucible
Fullness singing bells

LXXVI
Share with great people
Immerse within great ideas
Lambs sleep separate

LXXVII
Anticipation
The secret between both worlds
Blue ocean, green flash

LXXVIII
Soul sounds of Summer
Tweet, caw, screech, hum, buzz, meow, chirp
Between moons silence

Between moons silence

LXXIX
Truth beckons to you
Speaking who you are, always
Mountain presence be

LXXX
Rising sun in East
Walking vision of placement
Manifesting truth

LXXXI
The boon comes hidden
Seeping, attached everywhere
Wren song acceptance

LXXXII
Inspiration fire
Follow this gift of meaning
Burning life's desire

Inspiration fire

LXXXIII
Spark within the soul
Creative in survival
Water quenches thirst

LXXXIV
Fog ending summer
Gardens reveal all their truth
Abundance follows

AUTUMN

LXXXV
West wind of water
Opens outcome from silence
Of harvest wisdom

LXXXVI
The change of season
Adapting for survival
Turtles always home

LXXXVII
Cultural family
Supports new exploration
Albatross cliff dive

LXXXVIII
Hummingbird bridging
Joy from the past to future
Rainbows of nectar

Rainbows of nectar

LXXXIX
Allowing nature
Now, accepting your nature
Joining together

XC
Spoon and bowl await
The great fusion of culture
Together a soup

XCI
Black Ruby arrives
Announcing the feminine
Trusting again fully

XCII
Belly laugh resets
The world, heart flies to high branch
Breathing full open

XCIII
Crumbling stone, leaves fall
Living the death opens life
Breathe the transcendence

Crumbling stone, leaves fall

XCIV
Sky view constant change
Seasons, feeling, thought, action
Flexible in change

XCV
Sundown blue and gold
Sinking through time and the sea
Darkness rises quiet

Sinking through time and the sea

XCVI
Still light, cools, dampens
Nature simplifies, leaves fall
Life drops, goes below

XCVII
Wind, water, and stone
Listening for Ancient ones
Blackbird steps forward

XCVIII
Animals wander
Clear path offering no home
Searching loneliness

Animals wander

XCIX
Progress in the good
Persistence is step by step
Four leg migrations

C
Where is the red wound?
Carried through all our nature
Linking together

CI

Ascending mountain

Expanding perspective, now

Higher learning grows

Ascending mountain

CII
Nights golden azure
Seeping through dusk air awash
Plants turn to coolness

CIII
Love is at the heart
Near to where ever you are
Healing fire, air, stone

Healing fire, air, stone

CIV
You opened my heart
Breath passed mystery beyond
Why, why, why, why, why

CV
Holding all you have
Sun, moon, the stars, and heaven
Asking the question

Sun, moon, the stars, and heaven

CVI
The white flutter-by
Approaches itself freely
Capturing all sight

CVII
Her life goes below
Stirring leaves nudging of soil
Merging the One

CVIII
Do the necessary
Water flows, fills holes, movement
Renews abundance

CIX
Waiting vultures pray
Rescue of path to rebirth
Levitate vision

CX
View in the mirror
Swans drink in reflection pool
Honest depth of soul

CXI
Speaking our story
Reveals good, true, beautiful
Follow seasons growth

Speaking our story

OTHER POEMS

Raven Conspiracy

Opening my eyes to five Ravens,
outside my window.
Eyes closed, remembering a gift
a raven had presented years before:
witnessing a conspiracy of ravens, eighty feet up
in a redwood,
bantering back and forth, croaking, and cawing
their opinions.
Two ravens coaxing a third,
the appointed soul perched alone on a large horizontal.
Suddenly, it flapped, squawked and hung head down
from the branch.
More chatter until unexpectedly, seeking freedom
it let go...
I gasped, thinking of a falling child, not trusting.
That raven tucked like a speeding bullet,
dove headfirst, reached twenty feet above ground,
turned up into clear air, and giggled away.
Those aerobatic antics held in the imagination
of clear air,
leaving me in awe, grateful, a feeling of grace.
As I remembered my myth, the five came again
to continue the story outside my window.
Walking, hopping, and, being brushed away
by the wind,
scattered like leaves, imprinting...
the great letting go to trust the unseen.

Darkness

Coming from the deep womb of darkness,
how can I fear it?
Darkness my birthright
pregnantly waiting.
You darkness I came from
the deep womb of darkness.
Then it was warm and known
now darkness is seen as scary, the boogie man.
What is there to be afraid of, what is to fear?
The birthright, the birthday
the coming out into the light.
The darkness of only nine months,
now a lifetime of living in the light.
Do we miss it so much we are afraid?
Afraid to be clothed in darkness again
where we were fed, just being.
I want the darkness again,
not now like I have witnessed
but before the birth of the light
before all the struggle for air and breath.
I want the darkness to come back again,
I want to be held by darkness, as before,
equally ready for the light, held enough to be ready
for the bright lights, the action, the cameras,
the showing up fully lit with fire,
fire to hold the darkness.

There is not enough darkness to last a lifetime,
I want the dark and light as Holy friends
I want the darkness again
to sustain the brightness,
the fire.

Whales

Whales outside my window,
you are far from me.
The whales told me today
you put your toe in the
Mediterranean.
They felt your longing for me.
I didn't swim today
not wanting the whales
to feel sorrow, of my longing for you.

Time and Space

This is about Time and Space
A Time out of time, before time, in between time,
something like this time,
or before time began,
like right now.
It's about the time and space between raindrops.
The time between tipping your cup,
and when the warm liquid touches your mouth.
It's about the time between when the Heron drops from
its perch,
and its wings catch air.
The time between pressing the petal, and the vehicle
advancing.
It's about the time between out-breath and in-breath.
The space and time between footfalls.
The time between flicking a switch and feeling the light.
The time between ringing a bell, and hearing the
ding or dong.
The time between crashing wave and hissing retreat.
The time between morning sleep and
the spark of light that awakens conscious thoughts.
The time between feeling full emotion,
and the saline tears forming on your lid.
There is more in-between time than time, more space
that matters.
The Mystery gathers at the edge of our thoughts,
and insistently waits and listens for our noticing.

Dreams

The Sun didn't shine while you were gone,
only the moon
tide pulling emotion, ebb and flow,
You the dark mystery, ghosting my dreams
fleeing at dawn,
leaving me.

Those Persimmons

Those persimmons
hanging like small bright glowing lanterns, pumpkinish.
Leaves turning color at the same time
ripening and waiting,
birds and squirrels not waiting.
Thinking of you dried, in cookies, pies,
or fresh, crunching like an apple.
Oh, what a Christmas delight
starting after Thanksgiving.
I leave the ones pecked and sampled.
I saw you mother squirrel jump
from fence, to tree, to branch
on your hind legs stretching out grabbing the fruit
with both clawed hands
pulling and pulling while balanced on your hind feet.
Finally, the persimmon letting go for you.
It fell to the ground.
Now eating one face to face,
Your jaws moving like locomotives, pistons,
Chomping with determined speed,
Pieces of persimmon flying,
in all directions, like sawdust off a buzz saw.
Half-full moving to another branch
pulling another persimmon to the ground
leaving and coming back to retrieve
your fallen fruit filled with the sweet flavor of fall.

While leaves fall like soft rain
making art on the brown earth.
The shapes and colors, curved, flat,
each leaf curled, small, large, red, yellow,
green, gold, orange, as subtle rainbows.
All that beauty, all that beauty, going into the great
earth,
receding inside and going deep.
Restoring all that growth for spring.
The groundwork and death renewing
the strength to find myself again in this earth.

Broken Bird

This morning a broken bird on my path,
greenish, gray brown feathers
ruby, red crown
still warm.
I walked on but noticed,
the passing of a bird,
another messenger, called to higher duty,
What did the Great Spirit do
for the passing of one sweet bird song?

The Taste of Imprisonment

The taste of imprisonment comes from the mind
and the body's depository of wisdom.
The body feels limitation
begins to pace and see
the field beyond the gate,
the life outside the bars,
the lingering taste of metal on the tongue.
The touch of tongue to metal
to taste the bars of limitation, never forgotten
lingering in the memory of freedom.
The mind entrapped by structure,
imagined structure, trapped by routine, sameness,
the body pacing behind bars.
Mental imprisonment appearing real.
Lack of imagination over the walls of imprisoned being.
Mental walls of belief bring the mind to face
the stone wall of belief.
Seeing only stone not the face observing the wall.
Not seeing the whole life of who you are.
The wall or bars, or the taste of metal
are not you, but fear expressed in the thoughts.
The holding, a forgotten hurt, wanting safety,
release, freedom,
from the taste of metal.

Birds

I listened to the Birds this morning.
They were all talking at the same time,
and I thought I heard them say,
they loved me.

You Are the Mystery

No more complaining, you are the Mystery.
Creating out of Mystery, is a mystery
no more being less than
no more being infirmed.
If you believe there was a Jesus
and if you believe what Jesus said
then believe you can walk again.
You can become a new Mystery to yourself.
There are no limitations, Jesus and others have told you.
Listen as if he is sitting next to you in your bedroom.
He is occupying your spare room.
He has moved into that open space
between your ears and deeper
into your desperate heart.
Believe, you are now, a Mystery to yourself
your awareness open to all possibilities
awaiting your command
the whispered commands of your divinity
waiting for transformation and the deep intuition
that has suddenly appeared, now, in your heart,
that has always been open yet you believed differently.
Love your life as if a gift from a mysterious stranger.
Grow up...
Leave your childish behavior outgrown, and
unbecoming.
Implant courage into the fertile parts left in you.

Those are the places of salvation, new beginnings.
Don't listen to worn out anthems.
Listen to those that love and support you.
This is your time to create, to love you for you.
Care not for negativity, learn, listen,
make up your own mind.
Believe in harmony, create it.
Grow up and become
your North Star.

Whispering

The wind brings the whispering of trees.

Retirement Tea

I look at your smile
the white curving smile
of my white porcelain mug.
The first cup of tea of my retirement,
steamy, smile of my favorite warm liquid.
As I sit in the first day of my new life,
I imagine the family that has picked the tea leaves
that have arrived in my cup today.
A family from Ceylon whose youngest
child ventures forth on her
own two feet, for the first time,
walking to the fields to pick her first tea leaves.
I watch her small curling fingers
plucking small tea leaves at her eye level
coached by her mothers' deft hands
to choose wisely.
She cautiously drops this first leaf into the basket.
A warm smile opens her face
to an ancient awareness she learns from family.
Her father and brother have stopped picking
to watch and witness this occasion,
remembering their own time of beginning.
She squeaks a small giggle and the day begins.
Sitting at the table pondering the tea,
and my smiling cup,
I want to look forward to every day

and how I can take time to envision
the first step of a young girl in Ceylon
picking tea leaves,
enabling me to envision my own next step
in my new life.
To pluck an opportunity that is looking me
straight in the eye
and sheepishly, giggle with delight, at my choice.

TODAY

I had to plant something today,
to save my life, my new life.

I had to plant something in the ground,
the solid clay I came from.

I had to plant something for me,
to remember this new life,
and all the other lives that are not me.

I had to plant something that would grow,
to remind me there is always,
a place in the ground to be me,
and to know in that final moment,
to remember everything.

I had to plant something today,
to remember the tree of forgetting,
knowing that leaving will always
bring a remembering.

I had to plant something today,
in my conversations
to bring new questions,
to an old, dry, wilted pattern.

I planted my new life today,
tended, nourished, watered, and fed
in the ground of remembering to belong.

Shana – The Carnival

You remind me of being at a carnival in the Midwest,
anticipating and happy.
I'm thinking you look like a Saturday afternoon,
blending into evening and all that excitement
and wishing.
My clean shirt and wanting to get close enough
to smell your perfume.
You in your tennies and fresh.
Then the fear and pulling back
What do I say once I'm close enough to smell
your perfume?
Walking around the booths and games,
Drinking a soda pop, wanting to win you
a giant stuffed teddy bear,
just for you.
Intense wishes and expectations with you.
Looking at you like a carnival in the Midwest.
Lights, friendly people, buddies, classmates,
girls from other schools, neighbors, eating, watching
and just watching you with your tennies,
your tall body of grace.
You, even more like a carnival, yes, a dancing carnival
every step smooth, sure with your own expectations.
Walking to the edge of the carnival booths, rides,
and popcorn stands, behind the trees we go,
hand in hand, to steal a kiss.

Your warm hands tremble and hold tight.
Worth a whole year wait.
You remind me of a summer carnival day
ready to have fun, to cautiously explore,
all the ways you feel like a carnival.

Dreaming in Trees

Walking to the river
grandson asleep in his stroller
quiet forest, tiny wheels a rhythm of crunching leaves,
rolling gravel, smooth dirt, twigs crumbling.
A sleepy rhythm to keep the dream alive.
Walking, walking, walking, strolling, strolling, strolling,
the wind, birds, and breath
in and out through his tiny chest.
Fertile for the unconscious
hearing all the earth sounds, a walking meditation
mesmerizing this Buddha, breathing softly.
I stop to watch the moving river,
not to wake him from his appointment with the dream.
Letting more of this nature merge with his nature, a
bond.
Standing up, I move again, still asleep he is.
Then strolling again, he awakes…
"Papa," he says,
I stop and kneel down to him.
Just out of his dream, he motions above to the trees.
Looks up and points to the trees.
I ask, "Were you dreaming"?
"In the trees, in the trees, in the trees.
Up, up, up," he delights.
I see the god in his eyes,
I hear god through his tiny soft lips.

I feel opened, and opened again
to a precious life, to a heaven only now.
Falling in love again with now,
this now I see in front of my face.
I hear with all my senses.
I feel everywhere
now.

Paper

The blank white page,

A luminous, ghostly page of

waited beginnings.

Holding but not revealing,

asking to be who I am, not who I have been.

Waiting for the pen to paper touch.

A spark to ignite next steps to freedom.

Out of the bondage of inner thought,

to the bright beginning of a presence,

a word, a felt wisdom, expressed,

on this hollow, expectant, paper.

A declaration of what was, to what is,

for this moment.

Matilda and the Golden Finger

I sat down in my low camping chair,
my seat inches from the concrete floor.
Just finishing work with friends,
tearing down, preparing for new construction.
Relaxing, I saw an eighteen-month-old child walking
towards me.
She stopped, looked, and wanted to be with me.
I met her parents briefly during the day,
trying to remember her name,
surprised, I opened more and received her
listened and watched for an opportunity.
She stood against my leg and started to crawl
into my lap.
Parents and friends anxious about her vulnerability
watched. Mother wanting to protect her
We all watched her movements... gradually
I lifted her and sat her in my lap, the back of her head
on my chest,
she looking out at the building, friends
and family...safe.
We sat and I listened to make her comfortable,
I wanted to feel like her teddy bear,
her favorite toy, a bottle of warm milk.
I wanted her to stay as long as she liked,
The Truth was, I felt as though she was my teddy bear
my blankie, my comfort.

Soon, looking at the ceiling she pointed with a finger,
pointing out of her tiny cupped hand.
She began to say and describe
what she saw or felt, which I didn't understand.
Gradually letting go of everything and everyone in the
room except her
I began to feel some of what she meant.
Together as one seamless body, she laid her
head back further
her angelic face, facing the ceiling.
Seeing something, she spoke, her finger turning gold
gesturing to the large pointed sky-light.
Her lips turning gold as they expressed
seeing the Angels, and cherubs floating
in the golden hue of the light, pouring down
from the lit sky.
Genius pouring from her lips and her finger
lit with gold.
People noticing her emotion, her beauty shone with
a sweet passion
of knowing how to say her Golden words
from her Golden finger.

Mist

Today, mist and fog hung from trees
like Christmas decorations
expectant, pregnant with water.
Damp and moist nourishment,
the water, like liquid crystals
hovering in the space between trees
waiting to be drunk deep,
symbiotically joined, inhale, exhale.
The trees look at me and ask,
"Can you hear us drinking all this water,
this water suspended for us?"
They saw on my face that I did not hear their drinking.
"We thought you could hear us drinking,
because the whole of nature laughs at us
because we slurp and make all manner of sounds
as we drink."
"Stand tall, drink and feast."

The Moon and the White Buffalo

The White Buffalo standing
on the edge of a high plains plateau
searching the herd below
for the young and the old
the bold and the infirm
and those buffalo in the middle,
holding both extremes.
The light white snow mixing with
a flurry of wind, settling on white fur
holding in heat of a beating heart.
The White Buffalo standing in the glow
of the pale white full moon.
The scene of a thousand years
of roaming, now under this white moon,
reflecting the steaming breath of the herd.
The heavy heart of the white buffalo
beating for all buffalo, knowing the Great Earth will
provide
from the four directions,
the four seasons, the four elements,
the earth, the air, the fire, the water
all abundant in this place
under this quiet moon.

The buffalo white as the full moon radiating
the manifesting presence of the buffalo.
The white buffalo trusting
the moon and sun in their own roaming
through father sky, day by day
night by night, unattached in their heavenly path
reflecting the solid path of hooves on solid ground.
This holding of Earth and Sky
the white buffalo following the path
of manifesting the abundance of Earth.
Bridging the seasons, elements, the directions
through time and space, the known and unknown.
Witnessing this great animal and totem
choosing this place on earth
to merge white buffalo with white moon.

Vision Wind

Oh, spirit of the wind,
blow away all my chaff.
Leave only the seed of my knowing.
Let this seed grow in my heart,
that is full, open, clear, and strong with possibilities.

Oh, spirit of the wind,
Blow away the critical voices from my speech.
Become the breath for my new voice,
Speaking wisdom without right or wrong.

Oh, spirit of the wind,
blow away the weakness in my legs,
so I can stand strong in the force of adversity
and strengthen my leadership, step by step.

Oh, spirit of the wind,
Blow away the grey clouds in my vision.
Allow me to perceive with the eyes of Eagle,
to bring focus and clarity into my thoughts and actions.

Oh, spirit of the wind,
blow away my separateness from all things,
let me understand the mystery
and the secrets of each day.

Vision Quest, June 2012

**Awareness, Transformation, & Deep Intuition
Three Gates to the Creative Fire Within**

Afterword

Thoughts About My First Book

My teachers and mentors say that I have always been a poet, but it wasn't until the fall of 2017 that I read in Julia Cameron's book *The Artist's Way* about the "shadow artist" and realized that it was time for me to step out from behind being a shadow poet and commit, take a stand, and publish a book of poetry. I didn't know how that would happen at the time but I had undergone enough training in my master's in organization development plus many seminars in leadership, marketing, and many other disciplines that I felt I could create a book. I also felt it was time to trust the Universe and let go of how this creation might happen.

I had been hiding my voice behind other poets and memorizing their poems to read and recite at open mics. That step into freedom, the decision to publish the book was easier than I expected and was welcomed by my inner spirits, who said, "It's time." I started to compile all the haiku I had written up to that time, as I had learned from Angeles Arrien, Ph.D., in her yearlong classes in Sausalito, California, from 2004–2010.

I gathered other short poems together and started to feel into what it would be like, and what it meant for me to be a poet and writer. From scraps of paper and parts of journals and sporadic writing I had done, I began to gather the swirling and turbulent pieces of writing, like ocean gyres, that I had accumulated. At the same time my consciousness was also functioning as a gyre, as my mind began collecting the whirlpool of thoughts that were presented.

A small, critical voice inside was saying that the act of writing would be too hard and too exposing of my inner life. I thought it would be difficult to sustain the amount of time and effort it would take to sit and write, and write, and write. What I realize now is that this revealing of my inner thoughts and life in words is my salvation and a way to befriend myself. Rather than constantly looking outward for acknowledgment and recognition, I have found that exploring my inner world and writing has been the real revelation, a source of peace and grace. It has brought me a sense of peace that the outer world has refused to offer up.

I feel very humble at this stage in my life, especially, on the advent of this first book of poetry. Looking back, I admire many poets, and secretly aspire to be like them. Writers like Mark Twain and Walt Whitman are icons for me. Rumi and Hafiz are ancient reminders of how the human condition has not changed that much. Robert Frost and Ralph Waldo Emerson are early thinkers that expand how I think about life and my place in it. David Whyte, one of my favorites, has brought the mystical and spiritual elements of the natural world into my sight and soul. Billy Collins's humor always adds relief and a breath of fresh air, and bless Mary Oliver for her constant work of revealing nature's truest secrets to us. I thank all the poets in the world, published or not, who strive to bring their view of the world, their presence, and their voice into the known.

The bottom line of this endeavor is that I feel blessed.

The illustrations provided by Michael Hofmann, an artist who lives in Forestville, California, offer a visual connection to the haiku and bring life and flow to the pages. Through providence, I met Michael at the Pacific Zen Institute in Santa Rosa, California. I found that part of his artistic talent is in Japanese brush painting, which has an exceptional affinity with haiku. The feather that appears throughout the book floats with your consciousness and offers a way to rise above the gravity of your situation. The beautiful illustration of the feather symbolizes messages from your spirits, omens, the alchemical process to higher consciousness, and transcendence. The symbol of the feather supports the vision of seeing your life from a higher perspective.

My interactions with ravens have been important experiences that have shaped my relationship with nature and resulted in the title of this book, *Three Raven Gate.* One day, or "once upon a time" as the story could be told, I was at work and was walking toward a large group of redwoods. About eighty feet up in a redwood was a flock of ravens, also known as a "conspiracy" or "unkindness." I prefer to use the word "conspiracy," as it suggests their multiple character qualities. I remember there being five ravens, but there were three main characters. As I stopped to watch, they were croaking and cackling and making a furious amount of noise, flapping wings, and gesturing back and forth on the horizontal branches. Then suddenly one raven, sitting on a horizontal branch by itself, flapped its wings, rolled under the branch, and hung head down from the branch, wings tucked tightly to its body. Then without warning, it let go. I gasped, thinking of a falling child. The raven hurtled straight down like a speeding bullet, wings still tucked tightly to its sides. I just had time to catch my breath when, about twenty feet from ground, the aeronautic raven pulled out of the dive and flew away.

I had never witnessed such farcical activity in any bird and watching this scene, I felt privileged, as if it were a private show for me. The first poem in the book, "Raven Conspiracy," speaks to this experience. A few years afterward, I looked out a window at home and five ravens were again communicating and acting wildly. It brought me back to what I had witnessed and I wrote this poem to commemorate that experience.

It is not necessary to read this book from front to back, though you can proceed that way if you wish. It can also be used as an oracle and you may choose a random haiku or other poem as a guide for the day or for the moment. Trust your own deep intuition as to where and when to look for revelation and awakening. Let the haiku and other poems speak to you. This is for YOU.

Acknowledgments

In acknowledging this first book of haiku and other poems, I want to recognize the Great Spirit of creativity and imagination in all of us, including nature and all animals. I feel blessed to have awakened this knowledge of the creative spirit when I took my first pottery class at Luther College under Dean Schwarz, I realized I could be creative and had something in me that could create. This awareness and awakening surprised me, and I finally felt a mission or direction that I consciously acknowledged and pursued.

Dean introduced me to Marguerite Wildenhain in California, who taught pottery, sculpture, and hand building in clay during the summer. Marguerite Wildenhain was the first woman master potter out of the Bauhaus tradition in Germany. She taught pottery at Pond Farm Pottery in Armstrong Redwoods State Natural Reserve near Guerneville, California. To her, Nature was a great teacher of form and design, and her students naturally learned many life skills at her school. This was my first real deep dive into the creative process and learning what it took to become a craftsman or artist.

I want to acknowledge all the potters I met the three years I was taking classes with Marguerite, especially Larry Thoreson, and Peter Deneen.

Soon after taking pottery classes from Marguerite, I met a former potter and writer, Nathan McMahon, who has become a lifelong friend and mentor. He was instrumental in guiding me further into metaphysical studies and sparking my interest in writing and poetry.

The next influential teacher who appeared was the cross-cultural anthropologist Angeles Arrien, Ph.D. She was a gifted teacher, mentor, and friend. Her "Four Fold Way" program was focused on Nature and the four seasons and the right living that comes from studying indigenous cultures and their models. I studied with her for more than six years, and her work still echoes in my consulting, writing, and creativity workshops.

Nature continues to be my great teacher, and I am amazed at the spontaneous creativity that springs forth from this source. Nature nourishes all creatures. The seasons of birth, growth, fruition, harvest, and death and decay are always mirrors of our own cycles. We go through these cycles in our work, careers, relationships, and inner lives. Accepting these cycles of growth with grace goes a long way toward being at peace with our lives. I strive to acknowledge where I am in these cycles and adjust my patterns of behavior to be supportive of friends, family, and my community.

There are many poets and writers who have influenced my poetry and writing, so it is a daunting task to remember them as well as pay homage to their support and guidance. They are part of the seen and unseen forces that have shaped my writing. Marvin R. Hiemstra, David Whyte, Billy Collins, Mary Oliver, David Wagoner, Rumi, Hafiz, Christina Lloyd, Jonah Raskin, Larry Robinson, Ed Coletti, John O'Donohue, Rainer Maria Rilke, Robert Bly, Pablo Neruda, Joy Harjo, William Stafford, Gary Snyder, Juan Ramon Jimenez, and Wendell Berry have been guiding lights.

I want to thank my publisher, Waights Taylor Jr., for his help and guidance in getting my book published.

He is also an author, having written and published five books.

I want to recognize and acknowledge my ancestors and family that have fostered my growth and experiences. My parents Paul and Lou Jean Martens provided a safe haven growing up, which protected my late blooming.

I thank Erato the Muse of love poetry and Polyhymnia the Muse of oratory, sacred hymns, and poetry for their soft voices that offer inspiration and eternal fire to my poetry. One of my missions is to help people find their creativity within and bring it out into the world. More than ever, we need everyone's creative spirit in the world.

Finally, I want to thank all my friends throughout the years who have taken the time to help me, taken time to give me hints or suggestions on how to live an inspired life, and to those friends I haven't met that are out there ready to engage in friendship. Create and be well . . .

About the Poet

Brian R. Martens is a poet, writer, podcaster, and speaker, and he facilitates creativity workshops. He lives in Forestville, California, and has adult children, Trevor and Natalie. He has two grandchildren, three-year-old Jack and three-month-old Desmond. He delights in his grandchildren and is active in their lives. He is a California Poets in the Schools teacher and attends open microphone sessions as often as possible. He loves to garden, exercise, and walk in nature.

www.brianrmartens.com